Crypto Trading for Beginners

How to Earn Passive Income with Cryptocurrency

By D.K. Livingston

Text Copyright © 2019 D.K. Livingston

All Rights Reserved

No part of this book may be reproduced

in any way without the written

permission of the author.

Disclaimer:

The views expressed within this book are those of the author alone. The information contained within this book is based on the opinions, experiences, and observations of the author and is provided "AS-IS". No warranties of any kind are made. Neither the author nor publisher are engaged in rendering professional services of any kind. Neither the author nor publisher will assume liability or responsibility for any loss or damage related directly or indirectly to the information contained within this book.

The author has attempted to be as accurate as possible with the information contained within this book. Neither the author nor publisher will assume responsibility or liability for any errors, omissions, inconsistencies, or inaccuracies.

Table of Contents

Introduction 1
Technical Analysis vs Fundamental Analysis 6
How to Understand the Different Types of Candlesticks 8
How to Know the Price Range of a Trading Period 9
How to Know Where the Opening and Closing of a Time frame is 10
Candlestick Names and Definitions 11
How to Use Candlesticks to Avoid Losses 13
Candlestick Patterns 17
How to Know if the Price is Likely to Ascend or Descend 21
How to Use a Chart to See if a Trend is Likely to Reverse 24
How to Identify Buy and Sell Signals on a Chart 28
How to Determine How Far a Price May Ascend or Decline 30
How to Buy and Sell Bitcoin 33
Closing 34

Introduction

If you have ever struggled in the financial markets before, you were probably striving to find a solution.

You might have wondered what separates successful traders from unsuccessful ones.

When determining what makes a trader successful, there are a variety of factors that come into play, including:

- **emotional control**

- **risk management**

- **substantial amount of capital**

- **ability to identify intrinsic value of a company or asset**

But even if the above principals are utilized, the investors may still feel like they are going in blind. How does a person know when to buy or sell? How can an investor generate passive income with Bitcoin and other cryptocurrencies?

For example, emotional control can prevent a trader from jumping into an investment too soon. But how does a trader know when it's too soon? Or too late?

Simply purchasing and holding an investment for many years can certainly work, but the investor must be willing to deal with volatile market conditions during that time.

Using the *buy and hold* strategy, a person's portfolio can easily go up ten percent within the first month, but then lose thirty percent of its value during the next five months.

Since the investor decided to hold, the portfolio is now down by twenty percent.

Over the next six months after that, the portfolio might increase by fifty percent, leaving the investor with a thirty percent gain in a year.

A thirty percent return in a year is good. But why not take the ten percent profit before the profits diminish, and then get back into the trade with more money when there is a good chance that the bottom is in?

Getting in and out at the right times can allow the investor to use more capital on the next trade.

To illustrate using the above example, let's say two different investors are using $100,000 each to buy the same digital coin.

The investor using the *buy and hold* strategy will go from $100,000 to $110,000 in the first month, after the ten percent increase in value. By the end of the sixth month, this investor's portfolio will be down to $77,000, after the thirty percent decline from $110,000. After the fifty percent increase, the portfolio will go from $77,000 to $115,500. Satisfied with the return, the investor decides to close the position.

Now let's take a look at what could happen if the other investor exits and reenters at the correct times.

This investor's portfolio will go from $100,000 to $110,00 in the first month. Seeing that it's a fairly good time to take profit, the investor closes the position entirely. After avoiding the twenty percent decline over the following five months, the investor reenters with $110,000, then watches the portfolio increase by fifty percent over the next six months. After closing the position entirely, the investor is now left with $165,000, before moving on to a different investment. Now this investor has $165,000 to put into the next investment, instead of $115,000.

Both investors in the example started with the same amount of capital. They also bought the same digital coin around the same time.

But at the end of the twelve month period, one investor was in the green by $49,500 more than the investor who was using the *buy and hold* strategy.

A trader applying the *buy and hold* strategy might be very disciplined and unemotional in the marketplace, yet still struggle to produce the kind of results that are being sought after.

Commission fees will need to be paid to the broker each time a trade is executed, and those can add up.

But unless the trader is executing many trades in short periods of time, the fees are generally not expensive enough to justify a portfolio going into the red by thousands of dollars.

Of course, a trader can not be expected to "catch the exact bottom" or "hit the exact top" with perfect accuracy.

But knowing when a trend change is likely taking place can certainly help the trader make better decisions in the financial markets.

How can we know when a trend change is likely taking place?

How can we know when a stock is overbought?

How can we know if it's oversold?

How can we identify where and what the supply and demand is?

Market analysis.

Essentially, passive income is generated by doing some initial setup work. If done correctly, the setup work will pay off later on, with minimal maintenance.

Studying the intrinsic value of a digital coin, and then analyzing the charts from a technical standpoint can be seen as the initial setup work that can set the passive income stream in motion. Once the trade is placed, the investor can then allow the money to come in.

The amount of information out there is vast, and it can be overwhelming at times to decide how much of it is relevant to your particular situation.

Whether you are a short-term trader or long-term investor, using and applying technical analysis is important because you need to know when to enter and exit a position, regardless of the time frame.

Crypto investing can be largely passive, but it won't keep going in the same direction forever. If it's on a long uptrend, it will likely start a downtrend at some point. The investor will need to know when a trend change is confirmed, so a position can be entered or exited.

You can separate yourself from the crowd that simply buys a stock and hopes that it will go up. Technical analysis makes it easier for a trader or investor to have a plan, rather than just hold onto a security blindly.

This book will focus on the technical analysis information that is most important, as well as how to apply it to become more profitable in the financial markets.

It will cover:

- **How to understand the different types of candlesticks**

- **How to know the price range of a trading period**

- **How to use candlesticks to avoid losses**

- **How to know if the price is likely to ascend or descend**

- **How to use a chart to see if a trend is likely to reverse**

- **How to identify buy and sell signals on a chart**

- **How to determine how far a price may ascend or decline**
- **and more**

Technical Analysis vs Fundamental Analysis

There are some technical analysts who believe that fundamental analysis is useless for the most part. While they bring up some valid points in their arguments, it can be difficult to offer a definitive answer as to whether one form of analysis is better than the other.

Personally, I don't like to trade the financial markets without doing technical analysis, and I tend to emphasize it in my trading routine to a greater extent than fundamental analysis.

But let's review what both of them are.

Technical analysis: The identification of patterns and trends through the use of charts to determine which direction a security is most likely to be heading. This can be done by utilizing *trend lines*, *moving averages*, and many other indicators to locate popular price points for buying and selling based on what the security has done in the past. This type of analysis also relies heavily on price action and the measurement of volume of shares (or digital coins) being traded.

Fundamental analysis: The evaluation of securities by measuring their intrinsic value. Fundamental analysts typically try to stay updated on the latest news releases about the security. This type of analysis relies heavily on earnings reports, company management, and the shape of the overall economic environment.

Fundamental analysis can tell you if it's a good idea to invest in a certain company in the long term, while technical analysis can help identify a good time to get in.

A good company with plenty of potential is still prone to setbacks along the way. Some of these setbacks can be severe, and technical analysis can help a trader avoid large losses.

It's not necessarily a good time to buy just because you are expecting good news to come out about a company. Sometimes the price action does not reflect a positive news story that gets released, particularly if the security has been on a long-term decline.

Technical analysis does not allow you to see the future, but if used correctly, it can help the trader determine if they are paying too much for a security (or selling it for too little) at a particular time.

Generally, many investors and traders tend to agree that fundamental analysis should be used to determine which securities should be invested in, while technical analysis should be used to determine when to buy and sell.

Since fundamental analysis is rather straight forward, this book will focus more on technical analysis.

How to Understand the Different Types of Candlesticks

If you have not already decided on a charting platform to use, trading view is one of the most popular ones available.

After you reach the website, select the **Launch Chart** tab, which is located toward the center of the screen on the main page. By default, you will be directed to the AAPL (symbol for *Apple*) page.

To switch to a different stock, simply click the AAPL ticker toward the top-left corner of the screen. This will highlight it. From there, type in the stock symbol you are looking for, and then select it from the list that pops up.

Regardless of which stock ticker you decide to view, the trading view website should display a chart with candlesticks on it. The candlesticks that take up the bulk of the screen are the ones that are displaying the price action.

The bars below the price action candlesticks are there to display the volume of shares being traded.

Volume is certainly an important part of trading, but this chapter will focus on the price action candlesticks.

The symbol for Bitcoin in relation to American currency value is BTCUSD.

The symbol for the overall crypto market cap is TOTAL.

How to Know the Price Range of a Trading Period

When looking meticulously at a candlestick chart, you will probably notice that not all of the candles look the same.

Some of them might have long upper wicks, while others might have long lower wicks.

If a lower wick on a candlestick had reached a price point of $9.75, and the upper wick had reached a price point of $10.25, the trading range for that particular time period was $9.75 to $10.25.

By default, the *trading view* website will set the time frame to the *Daily* chart. To change the time frame, select the **D** symbol toward the top-left corner of the screen, then select the desired time frame from the drop-down list.

The time frames that will be most beneficial to you will largely depend on what kind of trader you'd like to be.

A day trader will open and close a position in the same day. A swing trader will "swing" a position overnight and will often hold onto it for several days or weeks. Someone holding onto a position for months at a time will generally be considered a long-term investor.

Day traders tend to look at the 5 minute and 1 minute charts the most often, while sometimes paying attention to the daily chart. Swing traders tend to primarily utilize the 4 hour, daily, and weekly charts. Long-term investors can benefit from looking at monthly charts and making decisions based on that time frame.

Determining which trading style is best is a matter of personal preference. Some people decide to stick with day trading because they find it very risky to leave a position open overnight. This could largely be due to the possibility of news coming out that could negatively affect their investments after the trading session. Many news outlets wait until after the markets close before announcing something that is likely to impact the price of stocks.

Passive income doesn't always have to be long term. Crypto can be purchased in the morning and sold in the evening of that same day, if that's what the setup calls for. In this case, the investor can do some technical research in the morning, place the buy order, and then leave the computer for the afternoon to pursue other activities. The investor can then return in the evening to sell for a profit. But again, that's what the setup would have to call for. There will be plenty of days where this exact strategy will not work out, but there will also be many days where it will.

I have tried trading on different time frames and have found my profit/loss ratios to be approximately the same, so it has led me to believe that swing trading is not necessarily more profitable than day trading.

How to Know Where the Opening and Closing of a Time frame is

The color of the candle will tell you where the candlestick opened and closed.

If the candlestick is red, that means the opening of the time frame was at the top of the solid candle body.

Note: a solid candle body does not include a wick. A wick indicates that the price did not stay at that particular region for very long. For example, if you are looking at a daily chart and a candlestick has a wick that reaches $5, but the top of the solid candle body only reaches the four dollar mark by the end of the trading day, that means that the price might have been trading at five dollars for a few hours or less, and soon went back down and eventually closed at $4. In this case, the high of the candle was five dollars, but it didn't stay at that price for very long, so a wick was formed.

The closing of the time frame happens at the bottom of the solid candle body of a red candle.

On a green candlestick, it's the opposite. The opening of the time frame happens at the bottom of the solid candle body. The closing of the time frame happens at the top of the solid candle body.

Tip: Some traders prefer to use black and white candlestick charts instead of red and green. The intention of some of these traders is to make the chart appear more boring.

When it comes to trading, boredom can actually be more beneficial than excitement and fear. Looking at the colorful red and green candles can stir up emotions more easily than the blander black and white ones.

Staying unemotional can prevent the trader from making irrational decisions that end of leading to losses.

If you are in a position, and you getting extremely excited when you see a green candle and panicky when you see a red candle, you might benefit from switching to the black and white candlestick chart.

Candlestick Names and Definitions

For a reference, here is a list of some of the common candlesticks that you are likely to encounter on a stock chart:

DOJI: Looks like a plus sign, a cross, or an inverted cross. The wick will take up the majority of the candlestick, leaving almost no candle body at all.

DRAGONFLY DOJI: A type of candle in which the wick takes up the majority of the candlestick and rests at the very top. It looks like the letter T.

GRAVESTONE DOJI: This candlestick looks like an upside down letter T.

LONG BODY/LONG DAY: A long candlestick. The majority of the candle body is solid, but has a small wick on the top and bottom.

LONG SHADOW: These are similar to the DOJI candles, but have just a little bit more of a solid candle body.

MARUBOZU: A solid candle without any wicks.

SPINNING TOP: As the name implies, this candlestick looks like a spinning top. It has a small candle body toward the center of the wick.

How to Use Candlesticks to Avoid Losses

Memorizing the names of candlesticks is not as important as knowing what they represent. The last section covered the definitions of some of the most common types of candlesticks.

Now it's time to understand how they can help you make more informed decisions in the financial marketplace.

But first, you will need to understand the difference between the "bulls" and the "bears."

Bullish market- this is when share prices are rising. "Bull" investors are buying stocks, believing that the share prices will increase.

Buying a stock with the intention of selling it later for profit after the stock goes up is called, taking out a "long" position, or "going long."

If a setup on a stock chart looks like it's calling for the price to go up, it is often referred to as "bullish."

Bearish market- this is when share prices are falling. "Bear" investors are "shorting" the stocks by borrowing them and selling them, believing that the share prices will decrease.

If successful, they buy back the shares for a cheaper price after the stock falls.

DOJI

The solid body is extremely small, and the lower wick is just as long as the upper wick, which means the buyers and sellers seem to be equally indecisive. This makes the trade increasingly risky because it is too unclear as to which way the market is heading.

$$+$$

If the candlestick looks like a plus sign, it's a good idea to stay out of the trade until more clarification is obtained.

If the candlestick looks like an inverted cross, it means the sellers were quicker to sell than the buyers were to buy. It's more bearish than bullish.

If the candlestick looks like a cross, it means the buyers were quicker to buy than the sellers were to sell. It's more bullish than bearish.

DRAGONFLY DOJI

$$\top$$

Since the candle body is all the way on the top, this means that the buyers were very quick to buy, which could be a bullish sign.

GRAVESTONE DOJI

$$\bot$$

Since the candle body is all the way at the bottom, this means that the sellers were very quick to sell, which could be a bearish sign.

Long Shadow

Since these candlesticks are so similar to the DOJI candlesticks, the same concepts apply.

MARUBOZU

A red MARUBOZU candlestick on a daily chart will open at the high of the day and close at the low of the day, which indicates that the sellers were in full control throughout the entire trading day.

A green MARUBOZU candlestick on the daily chart will open at the low of the day and close at the high of the day, indicating that the buyers were in full control throughout the entire trading day.

Since wicks are essentially nonexistent in this type of candlestick, it means the price action was very definitive.

If this candle is red on the daily chart, but the weekly chart recently had a series of green candles over the past month, this could indicate a good time to buy a security, as long as the candle is large enough.

The idea here is to find a stock that has been doing well in the longer term, but pulling back in the short term, so the trader can purchase it at a lower price. If it works out, the market will continue its upward trend after the sellers have "exhausted themselves."

If a stock has been on a long-term downtrend, this idea will be counterproductive. Buying the dip works fairly well in bull markets, not bear markets.

If a stock that has been steadily trending upwards for a few months suddenly encounters a five percent pullback in one day, there is a fair chance that the worst of the selloff is over, and if you are a swing trader, it could be a good stock to buy and hold overnight.

As a day trader, a strong hourly chart with a large pullback on the five minute or fifteen minute time frame, could indicate a good time to buy.

Picture it this way:

It's easier to preserve strength as a marathon runner than it is for a sprinter who is running at full speed.

A sprinter *could* surprise the crowd by continuing to sprint for a while, but generally, running at full speed is not done for a long period of time.

A large red candlestick is similar to the sprinters exhausting themselves, and if the stock has generally been bullish long-term, there is a good chance that the buyers will soon step back in to buy the "discounted" stock.

Even if this type of candlestick is technically bearish, since it is red and it closed at the low of the day, it can still indicate that it is a good time to buy, since the sellers are likely getting exhausted by using up such a large portion of their "selling power" all at once.

However, if the pullback is very drastic, such as thirty percent or more, this could indicate the beginning of a trend reversal, and this type of strategy would be negated in that case.

Look for a candlestick that shows a healthy pullback of approximately four to seven percent.

Another thing to watch out for is the history of the stock's price movement. If it is on a long-term uptrend, but has a history of pulling back fifteen to twenty percent during its rallies, it might be better to wait for a larger pullback before buying the security.

Long Body/Long Day

The strategy for the this candlestick can be mirrored by the same strategy explained for the MARUBOZU candlestick, since they are both so similar.

Spinning Top

A spinning top candlestick indicates indecision in the market. The price action is much less definitive with this type of candlestick because it shows that the buyers and sellers couldn't seem to make up their minds as to whether a stock was overbought or oversold.

It is often best to avoid making a trade when this type of candlestick presents itself because it is like flipping a coin.

The small candle body at the center of the wick shows that the buyers were very quick to buy and the sellers were very quick to sell. This can make it difficult to gain clarity as to where the market is heading.

Candlestick Patterns

The last section went over individual candlesticks. Now it's time to cover some of the common candlestick patterns and how you can use them to make more informed decisions in the financial markets.

Blue sky breakout

Generally, it's a good idea to wait for consolidation before taking out a long position on a security that has been ascending on the price charts.

But sometimes it continues to move up for several days or more, causing the traders who are waiting for an entry on the sidelines to feel like they are missing out on the big move.

In a relentless bull market, sometimes a trader is left with little choice but to jump into a security without waiting for it to dip a little bit.

A regular breakout is when a security breaks above a resistance level, but there are still more resistance levels up ahead. A blue sky breakout is when the security breaks through the final resistance level, leaving no other resistance points up ahead.

A resistance level is a zone that a security commonly gets rejected at, indicating that supply has exceeded demand.

During a blue sky breakout, you might see a series of green candles consecutively after resistance has been broken.

The trouble with blue sky breakouts is that by the time the security takes out the final resistance zone, it is usually already overextended, which could lead to a significant pullback.

If you decide to jump into a blue sky breakout, it's important to watch the trade closely, and not to hold onto it for longer than a few days.

One way of knowing if the security will continue to go up is by assessing how much follow through the stock has after it breaks resistance. If it breaks resistance, but only by a few cents, that's not very good follow through.

Cup and handle

As the name implies, the candlesticks on the chart will resemble a cup and handle. The cup will be on the left side of the handle and it will be in the shape of the letter "U," while the handle will have a slight downward trend.

As long as the bottom has a "U" shape, it is considered bullish, so it presents a buying opportunity. If the bottom has more of a "V" shape, it is best avoided, as per technical analysis indicates.

The candlesticks travel in a "U" formation. After making the "U" shaped recovery, they will start trending slightly downward again.

Picture a downward slope at the top-right corner of the "U." The buy signal is presented during the consolidation period of the slight downtrend after the "U" shaped recovery.

A realistic profit target can be assessed by measuring the distance between the bottom of the "U" and the top of the "U."

If the move from the bottom of the cup to the top was twenty percent, the profit target could be twenty percent, with a stop loss placed slightly below the handle formation.

One of the drawbacks to playing a *cup and handle* pattern is that it can be difficult to tell if the cup is truly presenting a "U" or if it is actually a "V." Sometimes a sharp, V-looking bottom actually plays out quite well.

Another drawback is that the cup sometimes forms without the handle.

Dark cloud cover

This candlestick pattern is made up of two candles; a red candlestick that opens above the previous green candle body, and then closes below the green candle body's center.

It shows that buyers had stepped in early within that particular time frame, but were soon overpowered by significant selling pressure.

Piercing line

A bullish formation with a two-day reversal pattern.

This happens when a candle is long and red, and then the next candle is green and opens at a new low before closing above the midpoint of the previous candle's body.

Rising three methods

This is where three short red candlesticks stand between two long green candlesticks.

It is a bullish sign because it shows that the selling has been minimal compared to the buying.

Falling three methods

This is where three short green candlesticks stand between two long red candlesticks. This is a bearish sign because it shows that the buying has been minimal compared to the selling.

Three black crows

A pattern that develops when three red candles are formed in a row, and all of them have relatively short wicks or no wicks at all.

They will open near the closing price of the previous candle, but as selling pressure decreases, they get pushed down further.

This is bearish, as it displays that the sellers have continued the downtrend for three candles in a row.

However, the size of the candlesticks should be taken into consideration.

If they are very small compared to the green candles before them, it could just indicate that the security is taking a healthy pullback.

Zoom out and look at the longer time frames to gain more clarification.

How to Know if the Price is Likely to Ascend or Descend

Although candlestick patterns can help you identify trend changes, there is still the question of whether or not the trend change is real or just a fake out.

Sometimes a trader will spot what appears to be a good opportunity to buy when the price breaks through resistance and begins trending upward, only to have the share price take a turn in the opposite direction and head back down again.

This is why knowing the volume of digital coins being traded in a given time period can be useful.

On a trading chart, the volume bars will be displayed toward the bottom of the screen. If you are looking at a daily chart, the volume bars will represent the amount of digital coins being traded for each particular day. If you are on an hourly chart, the volume bars will represent the amount of digital coins being traded for each particular hour, and so forth.

If bullish traders are looking to open a long position during an uptrend, they often like to see the bull volume increasing on the chart, just to give them the likelihood that the price of the security will continue to move up.

When bullish traders are looking to open a long position during a downtrend, they often like to see the bear volume decreasing, just to give them the added possibility that the downtrend might be coming to an end.

Picture the volume indicator as a speed gauge on a car. The car might still be moving forward in the intended direction, but if it's speed is decreasing, it is more likely to come to a stop.

If you saw a vehicle driving toward you on the road, and it went from thirty miles an hour to twenty miles an hour to ten miles an hour, you would probably assume that the driver was planning to stop the car entirely.

In the opposite case, if you see and hear a vehicle accelerating from down the road when a traffic light turns yellow, you would probably assume that the driver is planning on going through the red light.

As there are signs to look out for as a driver and pedestrian, there are also signs that offer clues as to whether a security price is going to continue increasing or decreasing.

Increasing volume is like increasing momentum. When the momentum looks like its drying up, there is a likelihood that the move is getting ready to slow down or stop.

In most cases, volume is strongly correlated to the size of the move on the price chart. The higher the volume, the higher the move in price. When there is a higher amount of volume than usual, the price will likely be more volatile than it usually is.

If you see low volume for days at a time, and then the security suddenly makes a move that is accompanied by a large spike in volume, it can be a good indicator that the move was for real and that the price action movement has a fair chance of picking up in the near future.

The same thing goes for day trading. If volume has been low for an hour of so, and then it suddenly picks up drastically on a fifteen minute chart, there is a good chance that the price action is on the verge of picking up.

If experienced bullish traders are waiting to buy a security on a pullback, but notice that the bear volume is increasing, they often see that as a sign to stay on the sidelines and wait patiently for a better time to get in.

Knowing where the volume spike takes place is another important thing to consider.

When a security has been trending in a certain direction for a while with increasing volume, and then it suddenly has a large spike, the trend might not be sustainable for much longer.

If a bullish volume spike occurs toward the top of an uptrend, it is often an indication that the trend is coming to an end. This is sometimes referred to as a "volume climax."

If a bearish volume spike occurs toward the bottom of a downtrend, it is often an indication that the trend is coming to an end.

How to Use a Chart to See if a Trend is Likely to Reverse

One of the good things about technical analysis is that you can identify supply and demand areas on the chart.

Supply and demand can also be referred to as support and resistance.

Support areas are known as places on the chart where buyers have a history of purchasing a security and moving the price up.

Resistance areas are known as places on the chart where sellers have a history of unloading a security and driving the price back down.

Certain support and resistance areas are stronger than others, so it's important to pay attention to the strength level of each one that is nearby.

Essentially, the more often a price gets rejected at a certain price level, the stronger the resistance or support area becomes.

If a candlestick for a security that has been trading at an all-time high reaches the $20 mark on the daily chart, goes back down to $19.50 the next day, and then goes up to the $21 range a day or two after that, the $20 mark did not prove to be a very strong resistance area.

If the candlestick gets rejected at the $20 mark many times, it can be considered a strong resistance area because sellers were usually quick to take profits when it reached that area.

Simply looking for bases of support and ceilings of resistance on a chart can help determine the supply and demand levels for securities.

One way to go about it is to count the number of times a security has touched a certain price point on a chart before it moved in the opposite direction.

But another way to identify supply and demand areas is through the use of moving averages (MA).

Since moving averages can act as support and resistance gauges, they are popular tools for traders and investors.

There are two different types of moving averages; simple moving averages (SMA) and exponential moving averages (EMA).

Although both of these tools are used to measure the movement of securities, they are slightly different.

The main difference is that the exponential moving average directs its focus toward current price action, which makes it quicker to react to price movement.

The simple moving average distributes its focus more evenly towards past price movement and current price movement.

To illustrate how a simple moving average works, here is a series of prices over a five trading day period SMA(5):

$5

$6

$7

$8

$9

Simple moving average calculation:

5+6+7+8+9 = 35

Five day period simple moving average:

35/5 = 7

The SMA for the five day trading period is $7.

When the price of a security is trading above a moving average, that moving average is considered a support area.

When the share price is trading below the moving average, the moving average is considered resistance.

Generally, the longer the time frame is, the stronger the moving average becomes, so a 200 day moving average would usually be stronger than a 10 day moving average.

To gain balance, you can use multiple moving average time frames on a chart.

For example, a trader might want to use a 10 day EMA, 100 day EMA, and a 200 EMA all on the same screen to get a bigger picture of what is happening.

If you are a long-term investor, you can use weekly moving averages or monthly moving averages on the chart.

To bring up the Exponential moving average on <u>trading view</u>:

1.) Select the **Indicators & Strategies** tab on the top of the screen.

2.) Type EMA into the search box and press the **Enter** key on your keyboard.

3.) The EMA symbol should now be posted near the top-left corner of the screen. Close the **Indicators & Strategies** window.

4.) Next to the EMA symbol, select the *Settings* tab.

5.) Under the **Length** section, adjust the parameter to the number you'd like to use. If you are using the daily chart, selecting the number "10" will display the 10-day exponential moving average.

6.) After setting the parameter to the number you'd like to use, select the **OK** tab.

If a security holds a certain support level for a long time, and then breaks it, that major support level can often act as a major resistance later on.

In bear markets, old support tends to become new resistance. In bull markets, old resistance often act as new support.

On the candlestick chart, the solid candle body will need to close below the support line in order to confirm that it has been broken.

If it simply "wicks" down past the support line, that doesn't necessarily count as breaking support because the buyers were very quick to buy. The close of the solid body of the candlestick is what matters significantly in this case.

Once the support has been broken, another thing to pay attention to is volume. If support is broken, but the volume is very low, the move might not end up having much follow through afterward.

How to Identify Buy and Sell Signals on a Chart

In addition to volume and moving averages, there is another common tool that many traders use to tell if it is a good time to buy or sell a security.

When a stock is overbought, that is often a sign that a trader should sell it. When a stock is oversold, that can often be a good opportunity for a trader to buy it.

You can find out if a stock is overbought or oversold by looking at the Relative Strength Index (RSI) indicator.

The numbers on the scale of the Relative Strength Index go from 0 to 100. On this scale, the number "30" indicates that the stock is oversold, while the number "70" indicates that it's overbought.

When the RSI on the weekly chart is oversold, that usually means that the stock has been in a long-term downtrend.

But if the RSI is oversold on the 1 hour chart, this could be a good time to buy if the longer-term trend has been upward.

When a digital coin has a strong daily chart, but an oversold hourly chart, that could be a sign that it is forming a higher low on the daily chart.

As long as the digital coin is forming higher lows and higher highs on the longer-term time frames, it is considered bullish. But it's usually not a good idea to buy a security when it's forming a higher high. It is often better to wait for a pullback, or in this case, a higher low.

To get the most out of the RSI indicator, it helps to review the digital coin's history of RSI levels. If the digital coin has a history of staying in oversold region for days or weeks at a time, it's probably not going to be a good idea to buy it as soon as it gets oversold,s since it hasn't been respecting the RSI territories.

But if a digital coin has been respecting the RSI territories by bouncing off of them, the trader should be able to make a more accurate decision based on the Relative Strength Index.

In a bear market, a security might trade between the 25 to 40 level on the RSI indicator's weekly chart for weeks at a time.

In a bull market, it's not uncommon for a security to trade between the 50 to 85 level for weeks at a time.

That's one of the reasons why it's important to know what kind of market you are dealing with. If it's a very strong bull market, and you are waiting for the RSI to pull back to oversold on the daily chart before you buy digital coins, you might have to wait for a long time.

If the stock has been very bearish on the daily chart, it won't make much sense to buy digital coins as soon as the RSI reaches oversold, since it can stay oversold for a while.

When different time frames start aligning with each other, it will improve the odds of a successful trade.

For example, if the 4 hour, daily, and weekly RSI are all oversold in a bear market, it could improve the trader's chances of making a successful trade if he or she decides to buy.

But even then, the trader will be trading against the trend, so it's usually better to be quick to take profit in such a case.

How to Determine How Far a Price May Ascend or Decline

An earlier chapter already covered how to know if a share price is likely to ascend or descend, but this chapter will cover how far it is likely to go.

Since moving averages can act as support and resistance, they will give a fairly good idea of how far a share price might go before it changes direction.

But another way of determining support and resistance areas is through the use of trend lines.

The idea is to draw one or more trend lines on the chart, usually one to represent support and another to represent resistance.

The resistance line can be drawn from the top high of a recent trend to the bottom high. For example, if a recent rally reached a high of $100 per coin and descended to a recent lower high of $50 per coin, the trend line can be drawn from the top of the $100 candlestick to the top of the $50 candlestick.

The support line can be drawn from top low of the recent trend to the bottom low. If the highest low of the recent rally reached $95 per share and descended to a recent lower low of $45, the trend line can be drawn from the bottom of the $95 candlestick to the bottom of the $45 candlestick.

Some traders prefer to ignore the wicks in this case and focus on the solid candle body, so the trend lines would be drawn from the tops and bottoms of the solid candle bodies.

When drawing a resistance trend line, it's important to make sure that none of candle tops are closing below or too far above it, as this would render the trend line invalid. Try to keep the price points aligned with the trend line.

The same thing goes for the support line. Try to make sure that none of the candle bottoms close below the trend line or too high above it.

The idea is to draw them further than where the current price is, so you can see where the price range might be heading if the trend continues.

After the trend lines have been drawn, it can give the trader an estimated price range of where the stock may bounce back and forth in.

For example, if the trend lines have been drawn from the candlesticks that are dating from five weeks ago to the current date, following the pattern of the trend line, continue to extend it to a later date.

If the security has been trading between $45 per coin and $95 per coin over the past five weeks, a trader can extend the trend lines two weeks into the future on the chart to see what it might be trading at if the trend were to continue.

After the lines are drawn out a couple of weeks into the future on the chart, the trader might find the support and resistance zones to be at $25 for support and $35 for resistance.

This can be used as one way of knowing what the resistance and support lines will likely be in the upcoming days.

The trend lines remain valid as long as the digital coin's price trades within that channel.

Of course, since this is like trying to forecast the future, these trend lines can break sooner than a trader might anticipate. They should only be used to gain a general idea of where the digital coin might be trading if the pattern continues.

To use the trend line feature in trading view, select the Trend Line tab on the left side of the screen.

How to Buy and Sell Bitcoin

After a fair amount of understanding of technical analysis has been achieved, it's time to get ready to take action.

One of the most popular exchanges for buying and selling Bitcoin is Coinbase. It is also one of the only online platforms that allows the investor to purchase Bitcoin directly with cash. It can also be sold for cash on the platform.

One of the drawbacks is that the choice of digital coins to invest in is very limited. Another drawback is that the fees are higher than other exchanges. But the beginner-friendly platform's ease of use seems to be worth it for some investors.

KRAKEN is another exchange that accepts cash in exchange for Bitcoin. This platform's fees are generally cheaper, and it also allows traders to "short" Bitcoin, but it seems to have stricter requirements.

Closing

Remaining profitable in the financial markets can be very challenging, especially as a beginner. But gaining experience and utilizing technical analysis correctly can improve a trader's odds of obtaining long-term success.

But you need to have a strategy and stick to it. Whether your strategy is to buy an oversold bounce and sell when the RSI reaches overbought levels, or to simply dollar cost average and hold long-term, it's important not to let emotions gain control.

A good way to take emotion out of the trade is to not look at it as making or losing money. Try to think of it as just numbers on a screen.

If many trades are being lost in a short period of time, it is usually better to simply stop trading for a while. Emphasize education, then start trading again, but with smaller share sizes the next time around.

Technical analysis is not magic, so it's unrealistic to expect it to play out as anticipated every single time.

As the market changes, your strategies might also need to change in order to stay profitable.

Passive income is not always entirely passive. The idea is to *minimize* the ongoing work process as much as possible, not necessarily eliminate it altogether.

Even though the owner of a business delegates the majority of the tasks to a group of employees, it would not be unheard of for that owner to stop in regularly to check up on things.

Staying disciplined and focused while trading or investing is critical, but if the initial setup work is done correctly, much of the income generated from cryptocurrency can indeed be passive.

www.ingramcontent.com/pod-product-compliance
Lightning Source LLC
Chambersburg PA
CBHW030737180526
45157CB00008BA/3216